GW00381822

Delicious meals from the golden age of rail travel

compiled by
Simon Haseltine

Illustrated with vintage post cards

SALMON

Index

Cover pictures *front:* LMS No 6220 "Coronation" *back:* LB & SCR H2 Class No 421 "South Foreland"
title page: GWR Castle Class No 7017

Printed and published by Dorrigo, Manchester, England © Copyright

LMS No 6100 "Royal Scot"

GWR No 6029 "King Edward VIII"

Cornish Riviera Express

First Class Dining Car Christmas Dinner Menu. Leaving London Paddington
in the morning and arriving at Penzance just 7 hours later, the Riviera Express
sped across Southern England taking passengers to their
Christmas holidays in the winter warmth of Cornwall.

Carrot, Coriander and Red Lentil Soup

**8 carrots (chopped)   5 oz. split red lentils   1 red onion (chopped)
2 pints vegetable stock   2 tsp. ground coriander   1 tsp. ground cumin
Fresh coriander (chopped, to garnish)   Salt and pepper (to taste)**

Heat a little oil in large saucepan, add the onion and carrots and sauté for 5 minutes until the
onions are softened. Stir in the spices and fry for a few more minutes. Add the stock and lentils
and simmer for around 45 minutes until the carrots are very soft. Leave to cool slightly, then
purée in a blender. Season to taste, reheat and serve with a sprinkling of chopped fresh
coriander. Serves 4.

Pan Fried Fillet of Scottish Salmon
with Shrimp Sauce

1 oz. butter   4 salmon fillets (skin on, thickly sliced)
Salt and freshly ground black pepper   ½ lemon (juice only)   Lemon wedges (to garnish)

Shrimp sauce:
3½ oz. cooked prawns (defrosted if frozen)   ½ onion (chopped)
1 clove garlic (crushed)   ½ can chopped tomatoes   Chilli sauce   5 basil leaves
Handful fresh parsley (chopped)   8 black olives (halved)
Olive oil   Salt and pepper (to taste)

To cook the salmon, melt the butter in a frying pan then add the salmon skin-side down. Season with a little salt and freshly ground black pepper and a squeeze of lemon juice. Fry for 3 minutes, then turn the salmon over and fry for a further 2 minutes, or until cooked through. Squeeze over a little more lemon juice, remove from the pan and set aside. Meanwhile, to make the shrimp sauce, heat a little oil in a frying pan and add the onion and garlic and sauté for around 5 minutes until the onion softens. Add the prawns, chopped tomatoes, a dash of chilli sauce, basil, together with a little salt and pepper and bring to a boil, reduce the heat and simmer (uncovered) for 5 minutes or until the sauce thickens. Stir through the parsley, and then blend with a hand blender. Ladle a little of the hot shrimp sauce over the cooked salmon fillets and garnish with lemon wedges and the halved black olives. Serve with French beans and roasted root vegetables. Serves 4.

Triple Chocolate Scroll with Cherry Confit

Chocolate scroll: 3 eggs   2½ oz. caster sugar   2½ oz. plain flour   4 tbsp. cocoa powder
1 tbsp. icing sugar   10 tbsp. chocolate spread (more if required)

Chocolate syrup: 2½ oz. caster sugar   2 tbsp. cocoa powder   1 tbsp. brandy   ½ tsp. vanilla extract
¾ oz. unsalted butter   ¼ pt. water

Cherry confit: 1 lb. pitted cherries   2 tbsp. light muscovado sugar   2 tbsp. red wine vinegar   1 star anise

Preheat the oven to 425°F or Mark 7. To make the chocolate scroll, cover a Swiss roll baking tray with a sheet of baking parchment. In a large bowl whisk the eggs with the caster sugar for around 3 minutes until pale and thick. Sift the flour and 2 tbsp. cocoa powder over the mixture. Using a metal spoon fold it in. Pour the mixture on to the parchment and spread it out into a rectangle about 8 x 12in. Bake for around 10 minutes until risen and springy in the middle. Lay a sheet of baking parchment on a damp tea towel and sift over the icing sugar. Invert the sponge on to the paper. Peel off the lining paper and trim off any crisp edges. Thickly cover the sponge with the chocolate spread. Roll up the sponge and filling from the long edge and hold the roll firmly for a minute or so to set in place. Take off the paper and tea towel, sprinkling the remaining cocoa powder over the sponge. Cut the roll into six slices and arrange on serving plates, spoon the warm chocolate syrup over the top and serve with a dollop of the cherry confit on the side. To make the chocolate syrup, put the caster sugar into a saucepan with the cocoa powder and water. Bring to the boil, stirring, and simmer for 2 minutes. Remove from the heat and stir in the brandy, vanilla extract and butter. Set aside over a low heat to keep warm ready to serve. To make the cherry confit, put the cherries in a pan with the muscovado sugar, vinegar and anise. Heat until the sugar dissolves, then simmer for around 10 minutes until thickened. Remove the star anise and cool before serving alongside the chocolate scroll. Serves 6.

LNER A4 Pacific No 60010 "Dominion of Canada"

London King's Cross to Leeds

Three-Course Luncheon Menu. Imagine travelling behind a streamlined A4 Pacific at over 100 miles per hour and tucking into a typical LNER menu using locally grown rhubarb from the 'rhubarb triangle' around Leeds.

Smoked Haddock Crêpes

4 oz. self-raising flour   1 egg (beaten)   4 fl.oz. milk and water (half and half)
4 oz. smoked haddock fillet   8 tbsp. mayonnaise   ½ lemon (juice)
4 tsp. anchovy essence   4 fl.oz. double cream   1 jar anchovy fillets   Pinch salt
Ground black pepper and salt to season   Paprika (sprinkle)
Brown bread and butter, lemon wedge and salad to garnish

To make the crêpes, combine the sifted flour, egg, a pinch of salt and sufficient milk mixture (leaving some to poach the haddock) to make a smooth batter. In a heavy bottomed frying pan, fry a portion of batter in a little hot oil for a few minutes each side until golden brown. Makes around 12 crêpes. Poach the smoked haddock in the remainder of the milk for around 5 minutes or until cooked through. Drain, flake and remove the skin and leave to cool. Next, combine the mayonnaise, cream, lemon juice, anchovy essence, salt and pepper to form a smooth paste and divide in half, mixing the haddock with one portion. Divide the haddock mixture between the crêpes and roll. Drizzle the remaining mayonnaise mixture over the crêpes, together with the anchovy fillets and a sprinkling of paprika. Serve two crêpes per person with the bread, lemon and side salad to garnish. Serves 6.

Apple and Walnut Strudel

6 large sheets filo pastry   3½ oz. granulated sugar   1 vanilla pod
4 sweet apples (a crisp green variety - peeled and chopped)
1¾ oz. currants and sultanas   3 oz. walnuts (chopped)
1 tsp. allspice   1 tsp. nutmeg   1¾ oz. butter (melted)

Heat the oven to 400°F or Mark 6. Meanwhile, take 2½ oz. of the sugar and heat over a medium heat in a heavy-based saucepan with the vanilla seeds for around 8 minutes, or until caramelised. Then add the apples, dried fruit, spices and walnuts and cook for a further 10 minutes until the apples are tender. Next, line two baking trays with baking paper and place a sheet of filo pastry on each of them. Brush with the melted butter and sprinkle with a little of the remaining sugar. Repeat the process so you have three prepared sheets of filo pastry on each tray.

Divide the apple mixture along the shorter edge of both pastry sheets and roll into two logs, tucking the ends in as you roll. Brush both with butter and sprinkle with the remaining sugar. Bake in the oven for around 25 minutes until golden brown and crisp. Serve with lashings of thick custard. Serves 6.

Ginger and Rhubarb Pavlova

Meringue:
6 egg whites   10½ oz. caster sugar   1 tsp. vinegar

Filling:
8 fl.oz. double cream   1 vanilla pod (seeds only)   2½ oz. icing sugar

Rhubarb compote:
1 lb. 1½ oz. rhubarb (washed and sliced)   2 tbsp. crystallised ginger (finely chopped)
3½ fl.oz. fresh orange juice   10½ oz. sugar

Preheat the oven to 360°F or Mark 4. To make the meringue, whisk the egg whites in a dry bowl until they form stiff peaks. Add the sugar a little at a time, whisking constantly and then gently fold in the vinegar. Line a large baking tray with baking paper and spread the meringue over to form a circle. Transfer to the oven and immediately turn the oven temperature down to 300°F or Mark 2 and bake for around an hour or until crisp on the outside. Meanwhile, mix all the compote ingredients in a large pan and bring slowly to the boil over a medium heat, reduce the heat and simmer for around 20 minutes until the rhubarb is tender. Set aside to cool and then chill in the fridge. To make the filling, whisk the cream, icing sugar and vanilla seeds together to form stiff peaks. To serve, spoon the cream mixture over the meringue and top with the rhubarb compote. Any remaining compote can be served from a jug at the table. Serves 4.

LNER A1 Pacific No 4470 "Great Northern"

Great Northern Railway

Two-Course Dinner Menu. Imagine yourself on the Great Northern Railway, travelling from York to London King's Cross, eating fresh potatoes, seasonal vegetables and milk sourced from Lincolnshire via the GNR branch line to Spalding.

Salmon with Hollandaise Sauce

4 salmon fillets (around ½ lb. each)   8 fl.oz. white wine
1 lb. onions (finely chopped)   2 bay leaves   16½ fl.oz. water
Salt and pepper   Bundle asparagus spears (trimmed)

Hollandaise sauce:
5 oz. butter (salted) (melted)   2 egg yolks   ½ tbsp. Dijon mustard
Juice of half a lemon   Salt and pepper to season

Place the onions, bay leaves, white wine and water into a large pan, season with a little salt and pepper, and gently heat on the hob until tepid. Add the salmon fillets skin-side down, cover the pan with foil and poach over a low heat for around 10 minutes. Add the asparagus and poach for a further 5 minutes until both the fish and asparagus are tender. Meanwhile, to make the Hollandaise sauce, blend the egg yolks, mustard and lemon juice in a processor and then slowly add the melted butter until well combined. Transfer to a bowl and season to taste. Place the cooked salmon on each plate, and drizzle with the Hollandaise sauce. Serve with the asparagus spears and buttered new potatoes. Serves 4.

Crème Caramel

5½ oz. castor sugar   6 tbsp. water   4 eggs   1 tsp. vanilla extract
1 oz. castor sugar   1¼ pt. full fat milk
Butter (softened for greasing)

Preheat the oven to 300°F or Mark 2 and grease the bottom of 6 ramekins with some of the butter. To make the caramel, pour the 5½ oz. of caster sugar into a pan and add the water. Dissolve the sugar slowly over a gentle heat, stirring all the time and then boil until the sugar turns a dark caramel colour. Remove from the heat immediately and pour evenly into the prepared ramekins. Set aside to cool and become hard, then butter the ramekin sides. To make the custard, whisk the eggs, vanilla extract and 1 oz. caster sugar until well mixed. Then gently heat the milk in a large saucepan until just simmering and pour into the egg mixture, whisking until smooth. Pour into each of the prepared ramekins until half full. Stand the ramekins in a roasting tin and half fill with boiling water. Cook in the oven for around 30 minutes or until the custard has set. Cool the ramekins on a cooling rack and then keep in the fridge overnight. To serve, loosen the custard with a sharp knife around the sides and then turn out onto the serving plate. Serve with single cream. Serves 6.

Metropolitan Railway

Stockbroker Breakfast. Opened in 1863, the Metropolitan Line soon spread north-west of London to the newly built suburbs of Harrow and Richmond. This typical breakfast was served on the line and enjoyed by the new and affluent breed of city bankers and stockbrokers as they travelled into the City to work.

Porridge

**1¾ oz. porridge oats   6½ fl.oz. water
3 fl.oz. milk   1 ½ fl.oz. cream   2 tsp. demerara sugar
Pinch salt   Honey (to serve)**

Put the oats in a heavy-based saucepan and add the water, milk, cream, salt and sugar. Then bring to a gentle boil and simmer for 5 minutes, stirring regularly. Pour into a breakfast bowl and serve with a good spoonful of honey. Serves 1.

Lamb Chop, Kidneys, Bacon and Tomato Grill with Anchovy Butter Dressing

4 lamb chops   8 lamb kidneys   4 rashers back bacon (thickly sliced)
4 tomatoes (halved)   5 oz. butter (unsalted)
1 can anchovy fillets (drained and chopped)   1 lemon
2 sprigs rosemary (leaves finely chopped)
Black pepper   Salt (to taste)   Oil (for frying)

First, prepare the kidneys by removing the core and slice lengthways. Place the butter in a bowl and mix in the anchovies, half the rosemary and a squeeze of lemon juice, then season with some black pepper. Roll the butter mixture into a thick sausage shape and wrap in cling film before placing in the fridge to chill. Meanwhile, preheat a grill and sprinkle the lamb chops, kidney and tomato halves with the remaining rosemary. Grill under a medium heat for around 5 minutes each side or until cooked to your liking. Serve with a slice of the anchovy butter on each chop. Serves 4.

Cocoa

Using a mug you will serve from to measure:
$^1/_3$ mug cocoa powder $^1/_2$ mug sugar (or to taste)
$^1/_3$ mug water (hot) $3^1/_2$ mugs milk
$^1/_3$ mug cream   Pinch salt $^1/_2$ tsp. vanilla extract

Combine the cocoa powder, sugar and salt in a saucepan. Blend in the hot water, mix well and then bring to a boil and simmer gently for 2 minutes, stirring all the time. Next, stir in the milk and bring back to nearly boiling point. Remove from the heat and add the vanilla extract and cream and then serve in mugs. Serves 4.

SR 5BEL No 2051 "Brighton Belle"

Brighton Belle

One-Course Breakfast Menu. Travelling on the romantic London to Brighton line, passengers dined in Art Deco carriages, and feasted on locally sourced kippers for breakfast.

Grilled Kippers

4 tomatoes (halved)   4 kippers   Unsalted butter
4 eggs (gently beaten)   Chopped parsley (to garnish)   1 lemon (cut into wedges)
4 slices of crusty bread (toasted)   Olive oil   Salt and pepper

Preheat the grill to high. Place the tomatoes on the grill rack, drizzle with a little olive oil, season well and cook for around 10 minutes. Then, add the kippers to the rack and top each with a little of the butter and cook for around 3 minutes until cooked through. Meanwhile, melt a knob of butter in a small non-stick frying pan and add the beaten eggs together with a little seasoning and cook over a medium heat, stirring all the time until scrambled and just set. Serve the kippers with the scrambled eggs spooned over the toast, garnished with the grilled tomatoes, chopped parsley and some lemon wedges. Serves 4.

LNER B2 Class No 423 "Sir Sam Fay"

Yorkshire Pullman

Afternoon Tea Menu. The Pullman Car Company was formed in 1882 to provide luxury travel across the UK mainline network. The Yorkshire Pullman linked London to the fashionable Yorkshire spa town of Harrogate, where passengers could enjoy taking the waters.

Dainty Sandwiches

Sliced bread (brown and white) – allow 2 slices per guest
Butter (room temperature)   Mustard and cress (cut)

Fillings:
Cucumber, cheddar cheese, ham, tomato, egg (all thinly sliced)
English mustard, pickle, salad cream

Butter each slice of bread and assemble your desired fillings. Top with the remaining bread slices and then remove the crusts and cut into delicate triangles. Arrange a mixture of sandwiches on a serving plate, ensuring alternate layers of white and brown, and sprinkle with mustard and cress.

English Scones

8 oz. self-raising flour   2 oz. butter (cubed)
1 tsp. baking powder   Pinch salt   ¼ pt. milk
1 egg (beaten with a little extra milk)   Extra flour (for dusting)
Strawberry jam   Cornish clotted cream

Preheat the oven to 400°F or Mark 6. Grease and flour a baking sheet. Sieve the flour into a large bowl and add the butter, baking powder and salt and then rub in the butter until the mixture resembles breadcrumbs. Add enough of the milk to form a soft dough and knead on a floured board until smooth. Roll out to ½ in thickness and cut rounds with a 3 inch pastry cutter. Place on baking tray and brush with the beaten egg and bake for 15 minutes or until risen and golden brown. Cool slightly on wire rack and serve warm with a dollop of strawberry jam and lashings of cream. Makes 6 scones.

Rich Fruit Cake

1 lb. dried fruit (sultanas, currants, cranberries, raisins and chopped dates)
10 fl.oz. cold, strong, black breakfast tea   8 oz. plain flour
5 oz. butter (softened at room temperature)   5 oz. dark muscovado sugar
4 eggs   1 tbsp. dark treacle   3 fl.oz. brandy   ½ tsp. freshly ground nutmeg
2 tsp. lemon juice   1 tsp. baking powder   4 oz. ground almonds
8 oz. candied peel, chopped   8 oz. glacé cherries, halved

The day before, place the dried fruit in a large bowl, add the tea and stir well. Cover and leave overnight. The following day, preheat the oven to 325°F or Mark 3 and line an 9 inch round cake tin with greaseproof paper. Place the butter and sugar into a large bowl and cream until smooth. Beat one egg into the creamed butter, then beat in a little of the flour. Repeat until all the eggs and flour are mixed together. Add the baking powder, treacle, brandy, nutmeg, lemon juice to the cake mixture and stir gently. Drain the dried fruit of any remaining liquid and add the ground almonds, glacé cherries and candied peel. Add to the cake mixture and fold in gently. Spoon the mixture into the prepared cake tin and gently level the surface. Cook in the preheated oven for 2 – 2½ hours or until dark, golden brown and cooked through. Turn out onto a wire rack and allow to cool. Serve sliced with a cup of Earl Grey tea.

SR Schools Class No 900 "Eton"

Southern Railway

Three-Course Luncheon Menu. The London and South Western Railway, later the Southern Railway, opened up holiday destinations on the South Coast and in the West Country. Rich in fish, cream and milk, locally sourced produce was enjoyed by passengers on these scenic routes.

Pea and Ham Soup

**1 ham hock   8 oz. split green peas
1 leek (thinly sliced)   1 onion (thinly sliced)
2 carrots (thinly sliced)   Black pepper
Dollop crème fraiche   Oil (for frying)**

The day before, soak both the ham hock and peas in separate bowls overnight in cold water. Sauté the onion in a little oil for 5 minutes in a deep saucepan until softened and then add the leeks and carrots for a further 5 minutes. Drain the peas, add to the pan and stir. Next, drain the ham hock and place on top of the mixture and cover with water. Season well with black pepper and bring to the boil, then simmer gently for an hour or until the peas are mushy and the ham is cooked. Skim off any fat during simmering. Take the ham shank out of the pan, cool slightly and carve into small chunky pieces. Remove around half of the stock and reserve. Next, blend the pea mixture and remaining stock, adding some of the reserved liquid if too thick, and then fold in the crème fraiche and ham chunks. Reheat before serving with chunky bread. Serves 4.

Sole with White Wine Sauce

4 fillets sole (boned)   2 tbsp. butter (plus extra for buttering baking dish)
¼ pt. white wine   ¼ pt. milk   1¾ oz. mushrooms (sliced)
2 spring onions (chopped)   1 tbsp. flour   ½ lemon juice   Salt and pepper to taste

Preheat the oven to 400°F or Mark 6. Place the prepared sole fillets in a buttered baking dish and cover with the white wine, mushrooms, spring onions and a little salt and pepper and bake for 15 minutes. Carefully remove the fillets to your serving dish, cover and keep warm, retaining the stock. Meanwhile, melt the remaining butter in a small saucepan and mix in the flour, then gradually add the milk, bring to a gentle boil and stir until thickened. Next, add the stock from the cooked fish and the lemon juice to the pan and simmer for a further 5 minutes, stirring all the time. Pour the sauce over the fish and serve with buttered new potatoes and French beans. Serves 4.

Bread and Butter Pudding

4 slices white bread   1¾ oz. butter (softened)
2½ oz. mixed dried fruit   3 eggs
10 fl.oz. milk   1 oz. sugar   ½ tsp. mixed spice

Thickly butter the bread and cut each slice into four triangles. Butter a baking dish and arrange the bread triangles in layers, sprinkling each with the mixed fruit and finishing with a layer of bread. Beat the eggs and milk together and pour the custard over the bread and leave to absorb for an hour. Next, sprinkle the top of the pudding with the sugar and mixed spice and bake in a preheated oven for around 40 minutes, or until well risen and golden brown. Serve with lashings of custard. Serves 4.

BR A4 Pacific No 60009 "Union of South Africa"

British Rail London to Inverness

Three-Course First Class Luncheon Menu. Speeding northwards, first class passengers enjoyed dining in the buffet car whilst the scenery of the East Coast Mainline hurtled by.

Asparagus Soup

1 lb. asparagus (finely chopped)   6 spring onions (finely chopped)
16½ fl.oz. vegetable stock (hot)   Salt and pepper to taste
4 tbsp. double cream   Olive oil (for frying)

Heat the oil in a large saucepan and add the spring onions and fry for 5 minutes until softened. Next, add the asparagus and cook for a further 3 minutes, then add the hot stock and bring to the boil. Simmer gently for around 6 minutes or until the asparagus is soft and cooked. Season to taste and blend with a hand blender until smooth. Stir through the cream, reheat and serve with crusty bread. Serves 4.

Steak, Kidney and Mushroom Pie

1 onion (sliced)   1 lb. rump steak (cubed)
10½ oz. kidney (ox or lamb – cored, trimmed and cubed)
8 oz. mushrooms (sliced)   1¾ oz. butter   1 tbsp. flour
10 fl.oz. beef stock   Salt and pepper   12 oz. puff pastry   1 egg (beaten)

Preheat the oven to 300°F or Mark 2. Heat the butter in a large frying pan and sauté the onion for 5 minutes until softened. Remove and set aside. Next, dust the steak and kidney pieces with flour and fry for a few minutes in batches until brown. Place the onions, steak, kidney and mushrooms in a pie dish and add the stock to just cover the meat. Cover with a lid and cook in a preheated oven for around an hour and a half. Remove from the oven and cool completely. Next, roll out the puff pastry to form a lid, lay it over the pie dish and brush with the beaten egg. Increase the heat of the oven to 450°F or Mark 8 and bake for 10 minutes, then reduce the heat to 350°F or Mark 4 for a further 25 minutes until golden brown. Serve with mashed potatoes and peas. Serves 4.

Fruit Flan

9 inch flan case (shop bought or homemade)
Selection of fresh or tinned fruit (strawberries, raspberries, blackberries, kiwi, peach,
mandarins – you will need around 5 cups)   1 packet fruit flan glaze

Prepare your chosen fruit by hulling and slicing in half, or by draining from the tin, reserving any juice to make the glaze. Arrange the prepared fruit in the flan case to create a colourful and symmetrical pattern. Make up the fruit glaze as per packet instructions and pour over the flan. Cool and serve with lashings of whipped cream. Serves 6.

Calendonian Railway Glasgow Express

The Mallaig to Glasgow Railway

One-Course Supper Menu. One of the most scenic railway journeys in the world, this started under the stunning wrought iron roof of Glasgow Queen Street Station and travelled north alongside beautiful lochs and rugged mountains to the fishing port of Mallaig.

Wild Scottish Smoked Haddock
with Poached Egg

4 smoked haddock fillets (around ½ lb. each)   Knob butter
13 fl.oz. milk   Freshly ground black pepper   4 eggs (to poach)
2¼ lbs. potatoes (peeled and cut into chunks)   1 bunch spring onions (finely chopped)
Knob butter   1 tsp. wholegrain mustard   1 tbsp. horseradish sauce

Place the haddock in a sauté pan, add a knob of butter, some freshly ground black pepper and the milk. Cover and simmer for around 10 minutes. Remove to a serving plate and keep warm. Simmer the spring onions in a little of the fish stock for a few minutes to soften. Cook the potatoes in a separate pan for around 20 minutes until tender, drain and mash with a large knob of butter and then fold in the softened spring onions, mustard and horseradish. Next, poach four eggs. To serve, divide the mash onto four plates and top with the haddock and then a poached egg. Garnish with some watercress. Serves 4.

British Military Train "The Berliner"

Sunday Roast Menu. The Royal Corps of Transport ran the military train between West Germany, and the British Sector of Berlin during the Cold War. With doors locked and carriages guarded, passengers dined on traditional British food during their four hour journey.

Roast Beef and Yorkshire Pudding

3 lbs. beef topside   1 oz. beef dripping   2 tsp. English mustard
4 oz. flour (for Yorkshire puddings)   1 tbsp. flour (for gravy)
1 egg   8 fl.oz. milk   3 fl.oz. water (for Yorkshire puddings)
2 tbsp. water (for gravy)   10 fl.oz. beef stock   salt and pepper

Preheat the oven to 400°F or Mark 6. Place the beef joint in a roasting tin and rub over with the dripping and mustard. Season with some freshly ground pepper and cook for 20 minutes per pound plus 20 minutes, or according to your preference. When cooked, remove the pan from the oven and drain off the juices. Cover the meat with foil and leave to rest for 15 minutes or so. To make the Yorkshire puddings, put the plain flour in a bowl, then beat in the egg and half the milk until smooth. Then beat in the remaining milk and water until the consistency of single cream. Increase the oven to 430°F or Mark 7 and pour a little oil into a twelve hole patty tin. Heat the oil for 5 minutes in the oven, then pour in the batter and return to the oven for around 20 minutes, or until risen and golden brown. Meanwhile, to make the gravy, skim the fat off the meat juices and bring to the boil in a large pan. Blend the flour with the water and stir into the juices and cook for a further 5 minutes. Add the beef stock and simmer gently for a further 3 minutes. Serve with the sliced roast beef and Yorkshire puddings, with roast potatoes an seasonal vegetables. Serves 4.

English Apple Pie

For the pastry:
8 oz. flour   5 oz. baking margarine   6 tsp. water   pinch salt

For the filling:
4 Bramley apples (peeled, cored and chopped)
4 tbsp. sugar   milk (for brushing)

Preheat the oven to 400°F or Mark 6. Sift the flour and salt into a large mixing bowl and rub in the margarine until the mixture resembles breadcrumbs. Add the water and firm up the pastry with your hands, until ready for rolling. Divide the pastry into two halves and roll out one portion until large enough to fit in an 8 inch pie dish and trim the edges. Meanwhile, gently stew the apples and sugar for around 5 minutes until they start to go soft. Allow to cool a little before spooning over the pie base and cover with the remaining rolled pastry lid. Press down the edges to seal and trim, make a small opening in the centre, and brush with a little milk. Cook in the oven for around 25 minutes and serve warm with lashings of hot custard.

SE & CR No 516 with a Royal Train

The Royal Train

Three-Course Dinner Menu. Taking the British monarchy between engagements, the royal family dined in style on game, fruit and vegetables produced on their various estates across the land.

Mulligatawny

**1 onion (chopped)   1 carrot (chopped)   1¾ oz. turnip (diced)
1 eating apple (diced)   1¾ oz. french beans (chopped)
2 tsp. curry powder   2 tbsp. water   2 tsp. tomato sauce
1 qt. chicken stock   1¾ oz. cooked ham (diced)   1¾ oz. cooked chicken (diced)
Pinch ground mace   Pinch ground nutmeg   Pinch ground cloves
1 oz. butter   Salt and black pepper (to taste)   8 tsp. rice (cooked)**

Sauté the onion in the melted butter for a few minutes, then add the carrots and turnips and continue cooking for 15 minutes over a low heat. Next, add the apple, French beans, curry paste (curry powder mixed with the water) and tomato sauce and cook for a further 5 minutes. Gradually add the chicken stock and spices and stir until the soup comes to the boil. Season to taste and gently simmer for 30 minutes. Remove from the heat and allow to cool, then blend until smooth. Add the pieces of cooked meats and reheat and serve with 2 tsp. of cooked rice sprinkled over each bowl of soup. Serves 4.

Game Terrine

**2¼ lb. lean game meat (select a mixture from pheasant, pigeon, duck, rabbit, venison – cut into chunks)   1 lb. 3½ oz. sausage meat   8 oz. liver (chopped)
10½ oz. streaky bacon (stretched)   2 handfuls fresh white breadcrumbs
1 egg   2 cloves garlic (chopped)   Pinch dried mixed herbs
Splash red wine   Salt and pepper (to taste)   Oil (for frying)**

Heat the oven to 325°F or Mark 3. Combine the sausage meat and liver in a large bowl and add the breadcrumbs, egg, herbs, garlic, wine and salt and pepper and mix well. In a frying pan, heat the oil and fry the pieces of game meat for a few minutes each side until brown. Next, line a loaf tin with the stretched bacon (leaving the overlap) and add a layer of the sausage meat mixture, followed by a layer of game. Continue with another two layers of sausage meat and game and fold over the bacon rashers. Cover with foil and place in a roasting tin half filled with boiling water and place in the oven for around 2 hours or until cooked through. Remove from the oven and press in the tin until cold. Slice into thick pieces and serve with cold toast, chutney and a side salad. Serves 6.

Queen's Cake

**4½ oz. butter (softened)   4½ oz. caster sugar   2 eggs
5 oz. plain flour   1 tsp. baking powder   1 lemon (zest)
4½ oz. dried currants   Splash of milk   Icing sugar (to serve)**

Preheat oven to 350°F or Mark 4. Line a 12-hole baking tin with paper cake cases. Cream the butter and sugar until light and fluffy. Then gradually beat in the eggs, then the lemon zest, sifted flour and baking powder, then stir in the currants and a splash of milk. Next, fold in the flour and baking powder until you have a gentle dropping consistency. Divide the mixture between the paper cases, filling each one two-thirds full, and bake in the oven for around 20 minutes or until golden brown. Leave to cool and serve with a dusting of icing sugar. Makes 12 cakes.

GWR Castle Class No 4073 "Caerphilly Castle"

Great Western Railway

Two-Course Luncheon Menu. Travelling on the Great Western Railway, often referred to as 'God's Wonderful Railway', passengers were often in a cheerful mode on what was also dubbed the 'Holiday Line', as the GWR headed towards the English Channel ports for ferry connections to exotic winter destinations in Europe.

Victorian Winter Salad

**4 hard boiled eggs (peeled and quartered)   4 sticks celery (thinly sliced)
4 beetroots (cooked and chopped)   1 red onion (finely chopped)
Bunch watercress (shredded)**

Salad dressing:
**4 tbsp. cream   2 tbsp. white vinegar
1 hard boiled egg (yolk only)   1 tsp. English mustard (prepared)
1 tsp. caster sugar   2 tsp. olive oil**

Fold together the prepared onion, celery and watercress in a large salad bowl and then garnish with the hard boiled eggs and beetroot. Meanwhile, to make the dressing, mince the egg yolk in a bowl and mix in the mustard and sugar. Then add the oil and cream and combine. Finally, stir in the vinegar. Spoon the dressing over the prepared salad and serve with chunks of crusty bread. Serves 4.

Milk Pudding

1¾ oz. short grain pudding rice   1¼ pt. milk
1 oz. sugar   ½ oz. butter (plus extra for greasing)
¼ tsp. ground nutmeg   jam (to serve)

Preheat the oven to 325°F or Mark 3. Pour the rice in a large buttered (around 2 pint) ovenproof serving dish and pour in the milk. Add the sugar and butter and mix well. Sprinkle with the nutmeg and bake in the oven for around 2½ hours or until a golden crust has formed, stirring twice during the first hour only. Serve with a dollop of homemade jam. Serves 4.

GWR No 6000 "King George V"

Great Eastern Railway Supper Train

Supper Menu. The Great Eastern Railway was the first to provide dining cars for third class passengers, where supper was served for workers heading to Southend-on-Sea for a much needed weekend excursion.

Herrings with a Mustard Sauce

**8 herring fillets   half tbsp. lemon juice   salt and pepper (to taste)
2 tsp. mustard powder   2 egg yolks   2 oz. butter   1 fl.oz. double cream
1 tbsp. chopped capers   1 tbsp. chopped gherkin   2 tomatoes (halved)**

Sprinkle the herring flesh with the lemon juice and season well with salt and pepper. Grill under moderate heat for 5 minutes on each side and then transfer to a serving plate and keep warm. Combine the mustard and egg yolks in a bowl and place over a pan of hot water and whisk until creamy. Add the butter a small piece at a time and whisk well. When the sauce thickens, remove the bowl from the heat and stir in the cream, capers and gherkin. Add salt and pepper to taste and serve over the grilled herrings with a grilled tomato garnish. Serves 4.

Great Northern Railway Co. Ireland

Three-Course Dinner Menu. Passengers travelled between Belfast and Dublin in the GNR(I) pale blue and scarlet livery with varnished teak carriages, whilst dining in style on 'Scotch Woodcock', a popular Victorian savoury dish.

Consommé Julienne

1 qt. clear chicken stock   2 carrots
1 stick celery   1 leek
1 small red onion   2 chicken thighs (cooked)

Prepare the vegetables by peeling and cutting each into 1¼ inch long matchstick strips. Cut the chicken meat into short matching strips. Now, bring the stock to the boil, add the vegetables and simmer gently for a few minutes until cooked. Add the cooked chicken strips, heat through for a further minute and serve with some French bread. Serves 4.

Scotch Woodcock

4 thick slices wholemeal bread   Butter (softened for spreading)
Anchovy paste (for spreading)   ¼ pt. milk
4 eggs   Pinch cayenne pepper   1 knob butter   1 jar anchovies (drained)

Toast the slices of bread, then remove the crusts and spread with the butter. Cut in half and spread each slice with anchovy paste. Next, add the knob of butter to a pan and melt. Meanwhile, whisk the milk, eggs and cayenne pepper, then stir into the melted butter in the pan. Heat gently, stirring all the time, until the mixture begins to thicken. Remove from the heat and continue stirring until thick and creamy. Dollop the mixture over each piece of toast and top with strips of anchovy fillet. Serve with asparagus spears. Serves 4.

Lemon Pudding

2½ oz. butter (softened)   6 oz. caster sugar
3 eggs (separated)   2½ oz. self-raising flour
1 orange (zest and juice)   2 lemons (zest and juice)
1 lime (zest and juice)   6½ fl.oz. milk

Preheat the oven to 350°F or Mark 4. In a large bowl, whisk the butter and caster sugar until pale in colour. Then, beat the egg yolks and whisk into the mixture a little at a time. Next, fold in the flour, together with the citrus zest and juices and milk. In a clean dry bowl, whisk the egg whites into soft peaks and then gently fold into the mixture. Pour the mixture into a buttered 3 pint baking dish and bake in the middle of the oven for around 50 minutes, or until golden brown. Serve hot with a dollop of thick cream. Serves 6.

METRIC CONVERSIONS

The weights, measures and oven temperatures used in the preceding recipes can be easily converted to their metric equivalents. The conversions listed below are only approximate, having been rounded up or down as may be appropriate.

Weights

Avoirdupois	Metric
1 oz.	just under 30 grams
4 oz. (¼ lb.)	app. 115 grams
8 oz. (½ lb.)	app. 230 grams
1 lb.	454 grams

Liquid Measures

Imperial	Metric
1 tablespoon (liquid only)	20 millilitres
1 fl. oz.	app. 30 millilitres
1 gill (¼ pt.)	app. 145 millilitres
½ pt.	app. 285 millilitres
1 pt.	app. 570 millilitres
1 qt.	app. 1.140 litres

Oven Temperatures

	°Fahrenheit	Gas Mark	°Celsius
Slow	300	2	150
	325	3	170
Moderate	350	4	180
	375	5	190
	400	6	200
Hot	425	7	220
	450	8	230
	475	9	240

Flour as specified in these recipes refers to plain flour unless otherwise described.